LILIES IN THE VALLEY

poems

Cedric Tillman
4/24/16

CEDRIC TILLMAN

Deborah—

Thanks for being here + for the
support! Blessings —

LILIES IN THE VALLEY

Editor: Randall Horton
Cover design: Aquarius Press
Author photo: Makia Tillman

ISBN 978-0-9897357-1-1
LCCN 2013954125

Willow Books, a Division of Aquarius Press
PO Box 23096
Detroit, MI 48223
www.WillowLit.net

Printed in the United States of America

Dedication

For Cleo and Linda Tillman, Ida Mae Diggs & Virginia Dare Tillman

This Little Light of Mine

Parables

The Ways of a Man

Thank You

Thank you Lord, for purpose & the paradigm of Christ; Patricia Biela, for taking interest; Randall Horton & Willow, for taking a chance; Daddy (for your example. for "choosing the better part"); Ms. Daily Word, aka Ma, for your example and hugs; Kia (You are beautiful, stubborn, forgiving & faithful. Thank you for our girls. I hope you can tell that I know more than I used to know. I ain't gone come to nothing 'til I do right by you); 'Rissy & Z (I hope I can help you find what you are here for, help you to remember in all you do who you belong to. Y'all are frighteningly smart interminably exhausting/remarkably cute/terribly loud); Damien (While there is breath, don't waste time—I love you); Yvonne & Giovanna Little (for encouraging me not to grow weary in well-doing; Nana—you are the sweetest mom-in-law in the world, thanks for everything); Na'im (I admire you and I love you); To Rev. Gerald Tillman (Aunt Linda), Jonathan Byrd (Ms. Queenie) & Dewey "Red" Tillman (Ms. Sarah) for generosity and kindness: I miss y'all; Thanks to all the aunts, uncles & cousins; Papa & Nana Moses; the Malloys, Tony Wilson & Alonzo Parsons (since Lilesville).

Thanks to (virtually) all my teachers, especially Ms. Hastings/Carlton/White. Ms. Wildman ("do you know, young man, that you have a gorgeous smile?") Scott Stein, Nancy Payne & Cynthia Furr (We all miss you so much); Dr. R.A. Shoaf (UF) for making me want to be that smart one day. UNCC: Dr. James McGavran, Dr. Jeffrey Leak for a timely word of reassurance, & Dr. Malin Pereira, for encouragement, interest, & advocacy. American U.: Nicki Miller, Profs. David Pike, Keith Leonard, Kermit Moyer & Myra Sklarew. Myra, thank you for your attention & convincing me that the work would be as good as the time I put into it. AU classmates: the aptly named E. Golden, P. Beete (hugs), V. Thrash (miss you), G. Belfiglio, Derrick Brown (QC!) T. Arthur (miss you), S. Beasley for motivation (5011 books), Corey & Tara West. Thanks to the UF fam for friendship & support: Dan & Kahrma Wright, Larry & Nikisha Baker, A. Lee, A. Speights, S. Bridges, J. Smith, W. Smith, K. Sawyer. Thanks to all the ministers I've learned from. To Mrs. Eleanor Washington, choir director at Rod of God Ministries ("Tillman, come up front with the sopranos.")

To the 'hood for making me tougher than I look—Archdale, Nations Ford, Olympic High. Antoine Mitchell (see you soon big bruh), Stukes Lemon (thanks for all the advice that only applies to me & not you, ha), D. Boyd, Kiwi, Amy Blanford & family, Rev. Michael Marsh (proud of you), Katie Becker-love you girl. Do it.

Thanks to D. Bankhead, L. Harbar, Penny Sowards, J. Tesch, B. Johncox, & R. Thermil for work (Leon: thanks for the Bukowski). Thanks to Katie McKiever for that laugh and for happening upon *Kakalak*, Tamryn Spruill, Sosha & Tony Lewis (for sharing Tony and holding the Firefly over 'til the next times).

Thanks to Cornelius Eady, Toi Derricotte, Alison Meyers, Sarah Micklem, & Cave Canem for the space and time that made so much of this book possible, the opportunity to learn from such accomplished writers, and the company of such talented poets. Robert R. Reese-love you man. Thanks to B. Gilmore (FB convo) & Colleen McElroy ("A poem can be about anything.")

Thanks for inspiration to all the Quiet Storm DJs, good soul music, Marvin Gaye, Donny Hathaway, Charlotte (Jodeci, Anthony Hamilton, Calvin Richardson) & all the girls I've loved before . . .

Cedric

Acknowledgments

Grateful acknowledgment is made to the editors of the following publications, where earlier versions of several of the following poems were previously published:

"Pretty Woman" & "something for the road" appear in *Cave Canem Anthology XII.*

"Virginia Dare" appears in *Cave Canem Anthology XIII.*

"Half-a-House" & "Other Woman Blues" appear in *The Chemistry of Color: Cave Canem South Poets Respond to Art.*

"Branding" appears in *Crosscut.*

"Holes" appears in *The Drunken Boat.*

"Mistress Summer" appears in *Folio.*

"Having a Form of Godliness" appears in *Inspirit.*

"Tact," "Your David, My Saul," & "A Few Years In" appear *in Home Is Where: An Anthology Of African American Poets From The Carolinas.*

"Read This Back," "...better yet, newlyweds," & "Ram in the Bush: Mr. Sturdivant's Story" appear in *Kakalak 2006: An Anthology of Carolina Poets, Kakalak 2007,* and *Kakalak 2009,* respectively.

Sometimes I wish I had gone along with that gang, but I guess I am too much a moralist at heart and really want to preach at people in some acceptable form rather than to entertain them.

—F. Scott Fitzgerald

Let the current flow freely when you feel that it is the true current that is flowing... And if you cannot release your personality, what you write, though it be engraved in letters an inch deep on stones weighing many tons, will lie like snow in the street to be melted away by the first rain.

—from *Peter Wiffle*, by Carl Van Vechten

For all good poetry is the spontaneous overflow of powerful feelings ... it takes its origin from emotion recollected in tranquility ...

—William Wordsworth

One thing I've learned ... is that whatever shortcomings you have, people are going to notice them; and whatever strengths you have, you're going to need them.

—President George W. Bush

I thank the Lord that my voice was recordable.

—CeeLo of Goodie Mob, *"Soul Food"*

The stone that the builders refused is become the headstone of the corner.

—Psalms 118:22

I wanted to say what wasn't being said. I wanted to give people a real story. I wanted people to know people like me exist in the world.

—Nas

This Little Light of Mine

Naps

I.

I pull my hair out.
You can tell I must've struggled.
Right now there is a ball of hair
in front of the flat screen.
Between this aging computer
and the rummaging for words,
I had time to pull out quite a pile.
When I breathe hard the naps run,
and for a moment I think
the roaches have returned.

If I forget to shake my shirt,
a tiny dark avalanche
tumbles down the slope of my chest.
Thinking it's a spider,
maybe a black widow,
I get scared,
Self-flagellate in its direction,
holler out
"shit!"
in a distraught whisper.

II.

These naps is tight, like a strong hug.
These naps is the abominable snowman off Looney Tunes, squeezing
These are the footprints of affectionate satellites
that lustfully orbited a world
until they couldn't take it anymore
Fell in love, licentiously and wholly giving themselves up to gravitational pull after
forevers of desiring a sort of coitus
and the collision destroyed it all so that this dark trail, luminous through the dark-
ness only because of its durable, peculiar shine
is the only thing like a black box we have

The All-American

My mind is American. My thoughts are the product of my American breeding.

I.

I am an All-American boy
And I'm proud to be an American.
I am of the finest American stock.
Pure breed of those that bred me.
My black hair, my brown eyes
The way I see through Chinese frames
Into American mirrors
And Japanese watch faces, is beauty.

II.

I am a fan of every All-American team.
I am a fan of pure All-American teams.
From Day One I was the Cowboy fan
The Yankee fan,
The Carolina fan.
I am a fan of nothing ignoble.
I am a fan of the teams people like me
Should be fans of.
I am a fan of the teams
That a man would be a fan of
If he's been where I've gone.
If he's from where I'm from.
There are fans of other teams
And I cannot understand them.
I do not understand how you,
Other fan
Cannot want the win I want
For us.

III.

I was born in a hamlet.
In Rockingham my American mother
Her hair a science project mushroom cloud
Bore me to an American father
His hair a science project mushroom cloud.
I remember the nurse,

The baby blue of the thing
She cleaned my nose with,
Its rippled bulb like a seashell.
I remember my funny reflection
In her silver ball earring.
She sat me, new and viscous, in Daddy's lap.
He kissed me like I'd never grow.
He hugged me,
Held me like I'd never grow.
I shall never be so new in the coming tomorrows
As I was that day.
I am not perfect, and
I will not be refurbished.

IV

The Americans who go to church
Go to church with me.
I am Baptist.
I am African Methodist Episcopalian Zion.
I am probably African Methodist Episcopalian
Without the Zion.
I am non-denominational.
I stayed out of the closet the skeptics
Made me for their convenience.
I listened to them,
They forbade me wine,
They forbade me women,
They took in wine,
They took in women
They took in men
I am a Christian in America,
And I am very often tried
But rarely by a jury of peers.

V

I am not an Atheist.
I am not
An Atheist.
I am not an atheist.
I am not, you know what I'm sayin',
An Atheist.
But you are, an All-American.

I am not
Good at line breaks.
But you are, an All-American.
I am not Catholic.
I am not Catholic
But you are, an All-American.
I am not a member of the Nation
(They are Americans)
I am in the top one percent of their 85 percent.
Or in the top one percent of their 10 percent.
But that in me which would be 5 percent
Is ravaged by my pure breeding,
My cocky Americanism,
That happily pervasive disease
And my God is
The one I experience most
The one I know best
Until all else is hearsay, and pagan.

VI

The All-Americans won't tell me
What to say
The All-Americans will tell me
How I should say
What they think I should keep
To myself.

And we will throw 'bows
In the moulting pot,
Until whatever lacks virtue
In the *not yous*
And the *not mes*
Is sloughed off like impurity,
So that something like heaven
Is within reason, and the First Cause
Blesses the nation.

There's a Lily in the Valley (Ms. Tiney's Song)

there's some lilies in the valley
bright as the morning star

more lilies down here
than on the slippery slopes
of mount academy
thug hill
and kinte's peak combined

in the valley they got more tyler perry movies
than spike lee joints but they proud of both

in the valley they got dreads and naturals
in the valley there are perms but only good ones

in the valley the hair shops and liquor stores
are run by people born in the valley
who kin to people from the valley
who like people from the valley

in the valley there is no bulletproof glass

(there's peace in the valley)

in the valley they go to church
'cause they still more worried about Jesus
than the color he is in the stained glass

in the valley Jesus ain't black,
he Jewish like his momma

in the valley the Muslim brothers can politic
and build with you
even if you eating pork rinds

(there's love in the valley)

in the valley, if you walk with a pimp
you have made a conscious decision to do so
and don't mind being called on it

17

in the valley some niggas use the n-word
in the valley jeans come with belt loops
so everybody wears belts

in the valley the lack of thought police
can taze yo ass if yo draws showing
without a Miranda warning

in the valley Adam and Steve
takin' a long time to get used to

in the valley they think Steve and 'nem
stay up on the mountain
But they be in the valley too

in the valley they play john mayer & elton john
they like michael and george michael
they got chris brown and bobby brown
clapton and luther and read that street lit
they are very aware of the stink of their shit

they have never heard of eckhart tolle
there's joy in the valley

in the valley a picnic is just a damn picnic
that's all
in the valley the poetry girls will give you the digits
even if you didn't say "peace"
even if you don't snap

there's love in the valley
Bright as the morning star

in the valley they say the hill spirits
treat them like drink mixer
could annexation ?
engender some sort of Harmony
more lilies on the mountains
less swoon into valleys

Amen Amen Amen

Read This Back

When I get old, or if I get hurt,
Read this back to me.
Remind me that I saw it coming.

I knew I would not always be young beautiful and vulgar
when I was young beautiful and vulgar,
that I would not always want nourishment
(being unable at some point to keep it down),
I knew I would not always be moved to tears
by the aesthetics of a beautiful woman in my lap
and mojitos in our hands by a seashore,
I knew I would lose the hair
the wind used to run through in the convertible,
that my hands could slip off the wheel
into catastrophe, so happiness was never an emotion
I could feel by itself.
I always knew I might not know I was here
At any moment, not just at some disease's advanced stage
or old age.
If I die young
Say I was not like these people
Who blithely think they deserve life,
Whose loved ones rage
against something they don't believe in
when they think the moment was too short.
I was never owed any time
but what I got.

If I get old, remind me that I knew
my soul would attenuate and become shallow,
that it would slowly leak away
until it had mostly puddled
in some other place.
Read this back
when the dumbfounded drapery that is left,
Trembling in its readiness
for death's swaddling clothes,
is what you speak to in your ignorance
When you wish to speak to me.

If I am crying and complaining when you visit me
where I am finally wasting away
Do not have pity, but instead

do us both a favor.
Tell me to buck up,
Remind me that I preferred this
to a sudden death,
Lift my sick, cloudy eyes up to yours
and read me back
this Post-It note.

Portrait of a Family

I.

A tall, cool yellow man in a tilted hat
stands beside your dark narrow figure
as you reach down to keep
three sullen milk-eyed little boys
in the picture.

Your stubborn hair only half remains in a ponytail
and you stare into the camera,
eyes wearied with having just enough
but not so much
you could become the teacher you wanted to be
not so much
we can't see the bricks under the porch
in the background, not so much
you could stop the older girls from getting married
for a two-person bed
and a bigger piece of chicken.

II.

Nowadays you might justly fault America
for the fatigue in your face
perpetually trapped in the tinge of this snapshot—
find her guilty of pricking your fingers
and pocking the cotton
with bolls of your blood.
You might blame her for the belt welts
on the boys, the penalty Daddy exacts
for coming up short at the scales,
the cost of doing insufficient business.

You could find her liable for
the family's disposal to swift half-lives,
the babies too early or too often,
an arranged marriage with the land
and a man harder than the last breath
he sieved long ago into silica-scarred lungs,
The atrophied potential of your illiterate sons.

But someone would argue the point.
Someone who bought bootstraps

with inheritance money.

This is the fruit of your seed
that lies rotting in her fields,
or you might merely pity
this aversion to husbandry,
her lust for self-sabotage.

Virginia Dare* (for Grandma)

Perhaps it is a pardon to name a child
after the first fruit of scavengers,
those Englishmen

who found enduring fortune
in a black market. Maybe
it's just pretty or maybe

your parents got just enough book learning
to think of you like hope,
and named you with a prayer

for your colonized offspring,
that they wouldn't be lost.
Even in a colored schoolshack

you could fall in love
with the sunlit side
of an outcome.

----

*Virginia Dare (born August 18, 1587, date of death unknown) was the first child
born in the Americas to English parents, at the Roanoke Colony in what is now
North Carolina. An expedition sent to England to replenish supplies took 3 years
to return and there was virtually no trace of those that had stayed behind. The
settlement has come to be called "The Lost Colony."

Half a House (after Beverly Buchanan's *SC House, New Bull Swamp School*)

Really wasn't no house. Mo' like half a house. —Linda Tillman

I.

Beneath the tinny percussion,
rusty-springed mattresses
married to iron bedframes
swerve into rude angles of evasion,
scrape over the scrape marks
in the sunken wooden floorboards.
When the sky turns dark
over the stripped rows, the man
makes room for a flourish
of feed buckets, their open mouths
employed to catch any note
the roof can't hold.

II.

They can reach through the floor
for breakfast eggs,
and Mama layers new quilts
thick as the gaps
in the wood plank walls.
Windows teeming with frost
peer in at ill-fitted children
puzzled together in the night,
but even in the boys' bed
the sleeping bodies
negotiate easy treaties,
and nestle into ceasefires.

Rev. Henry, 1980
Matthew 10:32-39

By way of apology,
he had a double helping of Grandma's
collard greens. He'd only eat legs.
He held a drumstick so light on his fingers
you could offer him your Sunday shirt
as a napkin and wear it to work
the next day.

His grey crown, neatly picked out
and brighter than Glory
half hid a picture
of my granddaddy,
frowning and heavy-handed
in his overalls, long dead
from the gravel pit's dust;

In the den he crossed his legs
left over right, nodded at times,
held back the knee
with knitted fingers while his wife
spoke of Sunday School,
the Buds of Promise.
He sat starched over the lip
of the couch, waiting his turn

and when he'd *Yes Lawd, sweet Jesus*
sweet tea
just melted on the settee.
Mother
against father 'Gin,
he warned,
daughter
against mother.

Out beside the front porch,
beyond the roses of Sharon,
a burgundy Bonneville
steeped in wax and country sunshine
had bonded burgundy leather
shiny like it'd been baby oiled
and when it was in park the shifter

sat up on the steering wheel
pointing at the sky
like a crooked tree limb.

This was back when they made
preacher's cars in Detroit, when we
used to call Ms. Henry *the first lady*
thinking that's as close as we'd get.
I loved that car
and when no one was looking
I was toppling over,
practicing how to sit.

A Premature Elegy for the Big Three

Even at Aunt Easter's funeral the preacher was drivin' something called a Op-Tima. Rev. Parsons down at Pee Dee A.M.E. got that slick new Buick came out a couple years ago but ain't nobody driving them police cars no more and the nice Caddies cost so and got to where they was rounded out like space cars. I guess he call hisself tryin' to switch it up but don't nobody drive a Kia down here but country preachers who want a fancy grill with a good payment. Something that look European at Quarterly Conference 'side them city boys' Mercedes.

One You've Heard Before

The field ends at an embankment
with a right-of-way pillar below.
He looks over the highway
and surveys the bare white brick houses
on the other side, like Moses
at the border of the Promised Land.
He sold the land they cut 74 through,
that across the road
that the Sturdivants and those Bennetts
& Mr. Bill & Centenary A.M.E. Zion built
their places on.
He helped make the Pee Dee side of Lilesville.
He was light-skinned,
but some lighter-skinned education
and Grandaddy mighta been rich.

Other Woman Blues (after Calvin Burnett's *Other Woman Blues*)

I wish I could open
that fist balled up in his chest
wish I could cover these naked walls

pictures of me and him and a minister
our little nappy-head children

frilly white dress
and a three dollar suit

hot-combed and frowned up
eyes full of that first flash

Just don't see
what he wanna go and put over me

ol' hain't colored hussy
whiter than Chicago snow

Guess it's only too natural
walking on something the color of mud

see if she wax paper
his sweet potatoes

him and lil' miss
just enough titty to sag

I hope she in love
with what he don't do

I wish these Negroes
would sit still with something
long enough for they food to settle

Memory

Momma says he and Grandma
argued as long as she could remember.
And Grandma could yap back
like the best of 'em.
When she was 78,
he pushed her down the four steps
that led up to the front door
and put her in the hospital.
Next week she came to Bible study
and Ms. Johnnie said

Ida,
if you want
I got something that'll bark over here
and bite over yonder.
But Grandma said *The Lord'll judge*
between me and he.

It's hard to tell what bothers him more
The fact that she's gone
or that she was more fragile,
hard to say if he truly misses her
or simply finds life inconvenient
without her

Maybe the memories explain
this constant look of pain and frustration
as if he's trying to revise his life,
that black print showing
through his Wild Irish white-out.

Ram in the Bush: Mr. Sturdivant's Story

Oh, he loved to get drunk and wreck cars.
'Lin and them little boys lived there awhile
They wont old enough to piss off theyself.
Found some of that Irish Rose stashed
in a old folded mattress,
I guess they used to pour out a little and put it back
cause he get to drankin' and acting crazy
and you know Miss Ida didn't play that

One day he caught 'em messing wit' his stuff
and he grabbed a broom and went after 'em
and they was a' runnin
and she musta grabbed the mop
and went after him.
Boy that was a time.
I came in and the oldest boy was in between 'em hollering stop
and Miss Ida had the mop
and J. Hazel had the broom and I told him to go on with his self
and put the broom down
and oh Lord it was a mighty commotion
'til we smelled something burnin'
cause Ida had got too close to that big black pipe stove
they had in the kitchen and it got hold of that thick
quilt nightgown she had

Regrets

The tree that shadows his shed in summertime
bows slightly under the weight
of small nervous birds
in the top branches, stripped by now
into generous sieves of sunlight.
A few steps away, the rusted out trash barrel
smolders the last bit of a can of green beans
and a just-emptied buttermilk carton.

Head down, hands shoved into dungarees
he's worn for how many days straight,
he walks to the edge of the lawn
where the field begins.
Once it was plowed and furrowed
from here to the intersection of the old road
and new road, filled with watermelon and collard greens,
corn and snap peas and *okry*
Off in the bushy part that he never bothered
to cut down, what you call poke salad
grew wild and his children showed their *younguns*
when to pick it.

The field and the *younguns*
is all growed up now.
Grandma is gone,
and the old yellow man
walks the yard, kicking rocks
and leaving shallow scars
in the packed-down gravel driveway.

Now I Am Old

Psalms 37:25

The evening is hot and thick
but he barely sweats.
On cool summer nights
he might burn the gas wall heater on low.
Most days, one of his girls
or grands from over the river
come to check on him
but they never spend the night.

Everything Is New

Everything is new, the city went ahead
and sloped off the property line,
moved up the shed. Daddy you'd love it,
the new grass and all.
Your footprints are all over the yard,
all over each other
like links in the fence.
I can see you pruning the big ferns,
those new little oak trees
twining their way into the aluminum.
Not quite 8 a.m. on a Saturday
and I can't believe you were across town
waking us with the saw
like this is your house.

Kia took a picture of you
hands on your hips, watching me cut
my own grass for the first time. She was
all big. The baby came a month
after you passed. I guess you know all this.

The city must have put down something
for the mosquitos. The Herndons say
they used to put something down
every year. Not nearly as bad
as last summer. Had some people come
trim the trees hanging over the
Asian people's driveway,
went and got me a blower.
Every nine days or so now,
the grass gets up
but I don't get out there
'til the weekends.

You finally got around to that new computer
and didn't have it but a week.
How much time that old damn thing
took from us all.
It had to be you.
All these idle people running around.
All these extras.

keep it in the road

I steep the black tea for 6 minutes
because I like some bite
and I plan to use sugar. It's
all I can have as early as I go in.
When it's right, it makes me wanna
roll my tongue and smack
like I'm tasting myself,
so I do it.

It's just after 12 and I'm up
waiting for direct deposit,
the bimonthly progress report.
I keep logging in and out
but the last couple times
I've gotten an error.
Sometimes I lapse into misspellings
of my children's amalgamated name.
The mortgage is on auto-draft, the Citibank
is closed, its envelope sloped up against
the computer screen like a lean-to.
I used to owe six and now I owe 3.
The clothes I bought with the card
are too small now, spending their dotage
at Goodwill. Lately the CD money
is lunch money and my wife says
I have a gut pack,
that at least you can see
where the muscles used to be.

Last night, it rained about this time
and the window is clicking again,
tiny darts against the glass.
I turn the blinds and the window is wet
with winged insects. Carpenter ants
according to Google, with an appetite
for wood. Tomorrow is Sunday
so after church
I'll need to get some spray.

Branding

The plates of my daddy's chest
come together at a raised area,
an old place
that looks like a tectonic result.
The scar runs down,
brown, unevenly corrugated
ranging near the bowl of his stomach.
I think it helps him remember.

When I'm home
I spy on him from my bedroom window
like old times,
watching him mow the yard
I avoided.
Just now he pauses
to wipe his brow in the heat,
casually looking around
as if he heard something interesting,
and rubs his chest,
tracing himself along this straight edge,
searching like somewhere
there is a switch that will
open it all up again.

When he comes in
I ask if it still hurts, and he says
he hasn't felt that pain in years.
Quickly I circle him on my tiptoes,
removing random shards of grass
from his fro.
He pours a glass of his favorite
Tropical Punch Kool-Aid I made
and complains it's not sweet enough,
makes that loud noise
to prove he's drained the glass.
Then he laughs, ruffles my naps
like I'm much younger
and says
Stay out them blinds boy,
ya mama gone kill ya.

Retail

There Is Room

The lazy residents in my complex
just throw their trash at the foot of the dumpster.
Coming home from work, the wife alleges
she saw a rat,
a quick, hungry flash in the pile,
and promises she'll never go back again.
Though I dread the trip,
especially in this northeastern cold,
I linger five minutes around this browned-out,
heatless hearth, heaving into it
the dumb lifeless scraps
of someone who depends on others
to finish their work.
I have learned to be thankful for the handle-tied
drawstringed necks which make it easy
to pitch these bags that short distance
between the door and the concrete immediately below,
and imagine that the people who have left these here
are also the people who wash dishes
they eventually expect others to rinse.

The people who bring their trash here
do not work at a mall, for if they did
they could not be willfully ignorant
of the signs on these things,
which ask only that one close the door
until the compactor groans into function
and makes more room.
They do not think of the groundskeepers
who faithfully attend to this place every Monday,
who endure the summer stench,
or come to work obscured by a ski mask
and the smoky cadence of breath
in winter's cold.
They cannot know the appreciation of a
"thanks, bruh"
when he sees me throw in someone else's bag,
and do not care about the trifles he gets
for his role as dingi-fied priest,
offering up garbage to a soulless behemoth
as if to help its votaries, full of crap
and dressed in the purest white,

make that last immolating lunge
onto the altar.

Now, as I come in smelling my gloves,
My careful wife wants to know
what took me so long.
But someone must stand in the gap,
and I feel heroic,
as should the Latino guy with the mustache
down at the mall dock,
who stands between the no-smoking sign
on the wall and the compactors
awaiting the next bag,
an iron prod in his left hand
and a cigarette in his right.

Americana (for Tyson's Corner)

I.

The young woman,
her sheer green and gold hijab
curiously and intricately fashioned

wrapped around the hair
and flowing down to its light finish
over the back pockets of her True Religions

knows there is something to see,
that she is abundantly potted
at the ends of an Abercrombie rainbow.

She and her girls
each have at least one Versace bag,
She has four-inch heels
on her Christian Dior's,
A Louis Vuitton bucket,
Enduring the mall walk,
Faithfully pulling her shirt down.

She loves it here.

II.

Don't mess with the Asian dude.
His folded arms are warnings.
When he needs you
He will call you.
At checkout, he will be tax-exempt.

III.

Everytime she passes by,
Ms. Latina, her long black hair
pony-tailed out of the way,
teasingly hollers out a chapter
in the textbooks, like
"en el restaurante!"
This is how she shows compassion
For my broken Spanish.
I kneel in my dry cleaned khakis

to scratched-up plastic display cubes
Allegedly in need of Windex.
¡Tenga diversión! she yells happily,
disappearing beyond the big doors.
Beyond the big doors
Most everyone speaks her language.
The name of this place
is tattooed into their polo shirts,
inscribed above their hearts.
The day comes and goes
behind the public bathrooms,
in the corridors between the storage rooms
and the locker rooms, the nightly trash run.
This smell, the grunts of acknowledgement
to the janitors, the security officer's cigarette,
Come into me, are part of me now.

IV.

All roads lead to an anchor store entrance.
On the way, see our lives lived out
trying to play parts
we can't afford to dress for
to impress people who look the part.
I give congressmen the packing tips
I learned from a training video,
But I haven't been on a plane
In years.

V.

When the man arrives, he tells you what he wants.
Hey man, need you guys to really press this week.
Hey man, let's make these numbers, be really aggressive,
Probe the customers, let's sell 'em something,

Hey man, adequate signage is a must, no discounts.
Hey man, keep in mind the 1 percent commission
Hey man, need you
To shut the fuck up.

When he goes to the back
I come to the front
To stare at the passing traffic.
The dainty, fly ass Asian chicks

Oblivious in their hurried little heels,
Some thick, supercilious sistas
Who know more than I do,
With their legs that have seen places
And the scars to prove it,
The giddy white magazine mommies,
who make me wonder at these new hips,
is it genetic mutation
or just seatless jeans,
these legs
it seems they never played in.
All this I see,
and I fondle my wedding band
nervously.

Window Changes

Hello all!

I hope you all had a good February, and lots of hugs and kisses!
As we get into March, we'll want to transition into some St. Paddy's Day stuff,
and marketing has been hard at work (is there any other type of work?) on some
suggestions.

Firstly, we will put our Forest Green TravelWorks Titanium series in the main
window. You should receive hanging signage and 6 x 9 cards for the Lucite stands
any day now. Be sure to make this display "pop" with some of the microfiber and
canvas Kaitlin bags, especially the ones with the orange and green striping. (See
attached picture. You don't have to follow it exactly, just a suggestion.) Or maybe
throw in a few of the yellow packing folders by Raven River (for you Green Bay
Packer fans out there.) You'll also receive some wonderful paperweight clovers with
a wide base that can be spread throughout the store. Center these in the middle of
your low luggage risers where we usually make room for our product catalogs (so if
they're knocked over by the little inquisitive ones, they don't break, hopefully).

Your second window will feature the new spring colors (lime green, lavender)
of Aztec's handbag line. Perhaps you could contrast a lime grouping with extra
pieces of the green faux-croc ladies wallets by Costa, which we'll want to get rid of
anyway as clearance items. If you're sufficiently stocked, let's go ahead and double
expose them in the window and the clearance section so that we can get rid of
them faster!

Thanks guys! Call me at extension 5140 with questions.
And hey, remember the most important things…
Have fun! Teamwork!

Morgan Richards, Merchandising

Our Special Holiday Hours, 8 AM to 11 PM!

It was so early in the morning
he was amazed the alarm had gone off.
The new day moved back the curtain,
and having survived the blades in the blinds,
the scarred light rested stubbornly
in the middle of the headboard,
pieced together like shelves.
It ran down, slicing across his left eye,
and so he rolled onto his right side
so that he might more comfortably contemplate
feeling guilty for not being up yet.

He thought of his mother
and her maddening wake-up calls, which had been needed
to end the sacred serenity of his rest
on every week's day except Saturday. Back in high school,
her rude musical provocation to morning duty was
This is the day this is the day
that the Lord has made that the Lord has made
I will rejoice, I will rejoice and be glad in it
and be glad in it
Her admonitions were generally accompanied
by his tears of regret for the game the night before, perhaps,
or just the simple dread of routine.
At home, he had so often been pricked
by her voice, so mildly and devoutly off key.
Please stop Mama
please stop
Please stop, he'd say, getting up.

Please stop.
He sighs again at the bedside,
looking down at the carpet
like a precipice.
The slothful man, says the Bible,
is so lazy he cannot lift his spoon to his mouth,
but for God's sake
It's dead quiet,
the birds are not even singing,
and so he sits with his eyes closed,
shamefully imagining that if he has been left behind,
The Rapture might at least
be a break in the monotony.

And until his someday comes,
the grey will not be held back,
only guillotined at a different angle
when the blinds are turned,
and re-routed when he adjusts the curtains.
They'll never lie quite right
to keep out enough light,
and the red of the digital clock
will always be there
to tell him when to go.

Lady at the Wachovia Patio

This week's novel splays the picture
of a red-lipped blonde
in diagonal repose across the cover.
The reader sits as upright
as a compass needle,
thin hips teetering confidently
on the edge of an off-balance metal chair.
Under the table she crosses her legs tightly,
left over right
like a promise she's been keeping.
When she wears black stockings,
there is always the look of a dark cloud
around her ankles.

Behind her through the glass,
Wells Fargo has been giving out freebies
in Wachovia's atrium. She removes
a red and yellow bookmark scaled with
millimeters, places it on the table,
perches her paperback between
her left thumb and forefinger.
Today, once the rival for the affections
of Toni's lover is introduced,
she won't notice her arm is tired.
Her cigarette smoke will loiter when she exhales
until the wind opts for the corner
of Church and Third.

Next week the patio will be closed
for painting, work on the façade.
The lady stares straight ahead
satisfied that no one knows her business,
some distance from anyone who might notice
the constancy of her jheri curl,
or draw conclusions from the white sheen
of her forest green work suit.

Opening

For the manager who said "_____, are you in denial about being at work?"

the people with Credit come by
staring through the gate like prisoners
foot tapping with stares or glares
pacing the length of the storefront windows

I say
i'll have this open in about three minutes for ya!

then go to the back
for the one more thing to do

on the stool over the gift wrap table
I sit in darkness
fingers splayed over my eyes
praying for another day's plenitude
of forgeries
A reservoir of B.S.
that makes wearisome summits of inflection
sound like enthusiasm
not necessity

at 9:59
I shuffle to the circuit breaker
inhale   flip a switch
so that grey quiet is rent
by white noise

today is a sunny day
so much of heaven
through the skylight
and still decorum
demands its jaundice

Parables

Dog Days, or, injustice anywhere (after Michael Vick)

Summer heat matters not
to the army of protestants as they go down,
Moses-like,
past the clinic and the old mill.
Lumps of emotion swell the throats
of loyal petitioners, who abide gnat clots
and the zephyr of DEET.

Some sing, some whistle
the Freedom Songs of yesteryear's victims
and victim advocates,
Others stare down the route quietly,
Tunnel-visioned, teeth bared by passion
As they soldier on together
For righteousness.

"The Movies" with Buckley and Williams

Here's another movie
in which the browner people
are the spiritual people.
This is an old convention, one seen in films
such as *Imitation of Life* and *Driving Ms. Daisy*
and in the work of writers like Hemingway
whose infrequently occurring black characters
were generally wise. The white girl,
blonde, thin, happy and definitely better off
than her immigrant Indian lover,
has these opulent parents
who we know, deep down, must make
campaign contributions to Democratic candidates.
Her parents have "a place,"
perhaps in the Catskills,
given the movie's New York City setting.

Inevitably,
Gagan finds the religion-oblivious Jacki annoying.
Though Gagan is hardly a devout Hindu,
he feels he ought to have been less aloof
from his family and its traditions
after the loss of his father.

Jacki seems almost genetically incapable
of plumbing the requisite depth of empathy
for Gagan. For her, death is just that- death;
She wants him to move on
so that they can return to their extra-Indian,
Columbia University utopian urbaneness,
but he realizes only now that he's been a sellout,
ethnically derelict, initially afraid
to even introduce Jacki to his family.
Eventually, Jacki's Ivy-League, stock whiteness
is inadequate next to Gagan's latent but effervescent
brown spirituality, and we understand that Gagan
must leave her for a new flame,
a necessarily more Indian one.

Williams

But, you know,
after being inculcated with the notion,

with apologies to Lionel Richie,
that common ethnicity, not just love,
conquers all, Gagan's well-traveled
worldly Indian wife leaves him
for an old flame, a French guy,
which leaves the audience,
particularly, perhaps
The brown audience, wondering
What white man said he wouldn't green light this film
if good down home white heathenism didn't trump
brown Holy-Ghostness at some point along the way?
In the end, it's not just that the film succumbs to a
stereotypically Hollywoodish, nebulous agnosticism
(the audience *is* gently beat over the head
with a rhetorical God/religion-is-not-the-answer throw pillow
when Gagan's wife cheats on him
which is a topic unto itself,)
but it's that the story's resolution is false,
or at least untrustworthy
because it reeks,
because it is so redolent
with this sort of what might be euphemistically called
demographic determinism.

So cue the French guy Buck.
We didn't pay to make this movie,
And I doubt we will pay
To go see it.

Why There Are No Nearsighted Thugs

Really, what good is a nearsighted thug?
For sure, this is no problem
when the task is merely to cap the dude
who's spilled a drink on the Air Force Ones.
Issues arise, however,
when you have to pick a nigga off at some distance,
one who, as circumstance would properly warrant,
is in flight.

Think of those manifold times when the homies ride
on those *bitch-made* sets.
Not only does a bespectacled thug
lose a little something in translation-
he just isn't a *straight-up menace*.
How does he break the news to his *connect*
about his myopia
and even if he goes with contacts,
can a thug who must always be at the ready
really be encumbered by the patience & dexterity
it takes to properly insert them?
If a thug has the presence of mind
to forgo rims for Lasik, is he really a thug at all?

He is of little good but for the humdrum,
low-level brandish & threatening of the vengeance
others must properly see carried out,
or the generic, stupor-driven *licking* of shots in the air
out in an unkempt Section 8 backyard.
Generally utilized when precision
isn't a must, nearsighted thug
might be called upon when the crew executes
your run-of-the mill senseless shooting
into a crowd, as one might find at the club
gathering for the post-party
parking lot pimpin' ritual.
But anyone could pull this off.
This is thug life for dummies.

That old saw, the one about
dressing for the job you want,
must keep nearsighted thug awake at night.
Suppose you're a junkie-
The day after your dealer gets glasses that aren't shades

Isn't he, for all intents and purposes, a fed?
"What a ho ass nigga he must be,"
his customers will say aloud with impunity,
"comin' his snitch ass around this muhfucka
looking like a gotdamned schoolteacher."

There is a certain comfort level the average shermhead
should expect to have with his weedman--
and if you're a crack fiend,
how disconcerting it must be
to buy drugs from someone who looks like
They know better.
Even a gold-rimmed Gucci bifocal is a detriment
to the persona that is par for the thug course, and
how calloused we are to the quality-of-life concerns
of young men who can only see
what's immediately in front of them.

Thin Air (for Trayvon)

1.

It's probably better to run--
so there's someone left
to tell our side of the stories.

But I like to imagine that I am brave,
that I'll opt for the fight
if I am ever contentedly
minding my own business,
then hounded suddenly
by a man who is decent enough
most days, anonymously regressing
through life toward the mean,
with treacherous designs on significance.

2.

A couple rows back
a little girl says *mommy, I'm skeered*
the hundredth time.
I'm skeered Mommy Mommy I'm skeered

but of course we are all scared baby
though I would prefer your fears
I do envy
how your reasons to be afraid
get to differ from mine

I am scared of death, certain deaths
mostly a sudden falling towards earth
a violent loss of altitude in old turbulence
on my journey through this tense
persistent air, a fear of descent

because young men I know
collapse into complicit skies everyday
and I fear I am too much like them,
that I won't get to see much
before I land.

3.

everything is noticed,
if not inquired after;
everyone is touched
as we brush past the wind
in a hurry for impact

the blood is thick with conspiracy
and everyone knows
but not everyone can feel
so some people don't notice the virtue leaving
some people say what left wasn't virtue

4.

I live in America,
and I tell my son the street lights mean
I don't plan to see his mother flailing her arms
beyond the embrace of ushers
charged with keeping this much of us
out of the casket.

5.

The Black President pronounces it *Trayven*.
The name is off the tongue quicker,
the sound dies away faster,
but it's probably not another failed attempt
at establishing his American bona fides.
It's just the way he talks.

6.

we need to get to the bottom of it
have a full and thorough investigation
we have a criminal justice system for a reason
and I hope justice is served
it's in everyone's best interests
that this be dealt with in a timely fashion
so the public can rest assured
that law enforcement will palaver the etceteras,
ensuring that we can so on and so forth.

Having a Form of Godliness

This know also, that in the last days perilous times shall come. For men shall be lovers of their own selves…unholy…despisers of those that are good… lovers of pleasures more than lovers of God; Having a form of godliness, but denying the power thereof: from such turn away… Ever learning, and never able to come to the knowledge of the truth. —2 Timothy 3:1-5, 7

Like men making eye contact
the mood was unsettling--
Though the seats were soft
the yawns were audible.
We sat, only half-anticipating
and let the speaker talk
over our heads.

The veterans, they nod their heads
continuously in time
to the inflections of the preacher's voice
The amens become passive acquiescence.
Truth be told,
We all wanted to be elsewhere
Sitting in bonds, obliged to that crucifix
Called to account
Because we lacked the bliss of ignorance,
All of us burdened by the blessing
of belief in salvation.

And the choir can hymn
of the need for the knowing,
But we fidgeted nervously,
for to give up life's lusts
for eternal life
is like giving away everything you got
in the hope that someone you've never seen
will give you more than you had.

So slowly we press
toward the meeting adjourned mark
Content to call ourselves Christian
and approved in our study

But when we are asked to turn to Hebrews,
Many flip to the front of the Bible, thinking
Surely that must come near the beginning.

Cana
John 2:1-5

Jesus

My mother is generous to offer
what she does not possess.
What business is this of mine?

She thinks only of this moment,
Of how our cousin can avoid this shame.
Better that he be branded
With the miser's mark,
For history will remember this first miracle.
There will be enough cynics.

And yet even now
She whispers to the servant boys,
Points to me in the crowd.

Mary

30 years since the angel came to me
With word of this Redeemer, the assurance
That I would be a Godmother.

Now I am widowed and my eldest
defies me with coarse speech,
his sharp tongue swaddled in scorn.

Was he not nursed at my bosom?
Who could he redeem
If he were dashed against the stones?

Surely he will do this thing for me.
Today this water will be turned
Into wine, and she who was called whore
Will be chiefest among women.
I will surely be redeemed by our Redeemer,
Justified in the eyes of my brethren.

Tact

Phil says
so what happened
and Sosh goes
Well, my BP

Blood Pressure

was up
it hasn't been up
the whole time
and they told me to come on in

it's
they call it preeclampsia
high blood pressure
it can be dangerous
so they said she needed to come now
they tried to turn her four times
'cause she was breech

That hurt like hell

basically
she was butt down
and you know
they just don't come out that way

Phil laughed

yeah   right

and I was thinking
how she sounded like a pro
how time was
she might have said something snappy
like   well,
maybe whores' babies
come out that way
butt down
and I'm not a whore
you know, just as a joke
a little levity
amazing that she didn't even think
to say that

pretender

today has been a revelation.
war was a "judgment call"
all this time
but now it's the worst thing ever.

"Have you *seen*
Fahrenheit?"

You know it's over
when they won't lie to you

he had just wanted to see her.
when she got there
he offered to get her something
but she said no thank you
and when he offered some of his
she said I don't drink after people
but she used to drink after people
and sometimes
she would lick the bottle mouth
all slow and nasty and giggle.

she looks away
the street must be a carnival
people must be doing naked flips and juggling
his arm is stretched pleadingly over the table
he slips whipped fingers
under limp fingers
that guillotine into his palm
like his hand is community service

after four hot months
six weeks out of the whirlwind
and she's a regular Cindy Sheehan

Your David, My Saul (for Meka)

I Samuel 18

I.

At sunset I watch the legions
train slowly through Zion,
loitering in our narrow streets
like brash perfume.
That armor is a bulwark of commotion
that covers over the cries of boys
straddling mothers' hips,
their thick arms stretched out
toward your indifference.

II.

When you call me closer
I always pretend
I did not hear you the first time.
You beckon again
and though I am afraid
I wonder what would happen
if you could hear my music clearer.
But I cannot trust you.
Your hand hangs wearily from the bed
too close to the spear
So I watch you as I approach,
And even though your eyes are closed
I slide the spear away
so that I am between it
and you.

Sex In A City

A woman stares placidly at her bloody hand
where the knife made its sinister angling
into flesh, looks for reasons in the drop
falling now from the edge
of a Wheat Thins box flap.

Her gauzed palm on the sill,
She gazes out at the intersecting streets
crowded with cars
people only drive home for holidays.
There are five trees as far as she can see
like some kind of quota
I might paint, she thinks,
The sun won't come out all the way,
She notes there are thirteen separate clouds in the sky
though really the twelfth is just strung out pretty far

Three days ago a man she'd known before
fluttered by, kissed her where she overflows
the elastic, her smooth tan flesh perfectly extra
for his lips and ripe enough to suck until redness,
and she knew he was doing it
like when they were smaller and younger,
and oh he made her feel like a thin woman
who can't paint
Since then she hasn't heard from him
so she practices thinking of him
as just some dude

She'd rather lean on the sill
but her hand is sore and dammit
she's not going to stand here
presiding over the rigmarole.
She runs her fingers over her chest,
smoothes over the soft channeling,
notices out of the corner of an eye
the stillness of her sandy afro
in a mirror.
Abruptly she shakes herself, straightens her back
Somebody loves this skin, she recalls

Once a wordy lover, a poet,
told her that her tongue

tasted like ripened tamarind,
and she replied with an obligatory
you full of shit
but she kissed him with her hands in his hair
and giggled like a stereotype.
If not by Friday after work,
then not at all.

Times like these
she can smell the iron of the stud in her nose
The pies at the Jamaican joint
come to the window, make her say
goat with an accent.
His lips were at my navel for a reason.
She puts on her overcoat.
I like work, she says.
I know that if I go
they will pay me.

Holes (for P. B.)

I.

You say your father is fond of birds
and tends to air, that the arms
of your mother were like tethering
to a lodestar. Whenever you leave
you remind her that she is a place
you'll need to come back to,
that you never intended
to leave her rounded and empty.

You write to make her understand
what friends see in you to embrace,
to show a father in flight how lovers
reanimate the skin and linger
over the soft places.
You write and become so gourded
your skin is a hollow moan
in the wind.

II.

Sometimes loving our parents
means remembering what not to mention,
to pretend you've forgotten the times
they picked at your scar tissue
because it loved you enough
to cover the wounds.
I have never been so sure
of how easy it is to redden--
your words make me wonder
at how I am tender to the touch
in a different place, all the ways
I can be pushed through
at some other emotion

so when I heard you today
and hugged you
and kissed your hair
I wanted to tell you how
the longing in your voice
brought me to this shattering point,
confess to you that I did not know

how anyone could look at you
like you weren't saying a thing,
as if your lips were moving
but your notes were too high,
when they stand within earshot
of kinship.

Rape

that afternoon the rainclouds happened by
like gaffers to muffle the sunlight
and there's something about when it's raining
the wind strong enough to blow raindrops
through the screen onto the sill
of an open window
I loved especially the gusts that blew wet beyond us
onto the green-tiled floor
and how it felt to kiss your cheek
and then your lips   using my hands
to catch what dripped over the V
of your sundress
cupping my hands for kisses
my hands underneath
like a balance
like a rapist

and like a rapist
I ask about condoms
and like a rape victim
you whisper
"On the desk"

"say again?"

"On the desk"
never could've imagined
rapist

and then wind
staring disbelief through the window
into heaven's blandness
sipping you like water
The rhythm of your breathing
the rain
and the rape

then you weren't really there
something about
the nyquil on your nightstand
or how I was best friends
with your ex-man
But if it wasn't for our joined hands

My little leap never could've
Pulled you over that ledge

And I think about others
who were persuaded
who eventually succumbed
and I wonder if the other women I raped
just never told
or convinced themselves
that when I rape
I rape respectfully
that when I invade
I violate in peace

The Secret

It need not be true, this idea you have
that you have something special to say,
that only you could put new drink
in the old wineskins
of these trampled themes.
It might not be true,
but you have to believe it.

And then you must put forth an effort.
You cannot teetotal during the glut.
You must be willing to move
when you are moved,
or stare patiently into space
until it comes.

It helps to be so human
that you need to lie a little.
Confusion is where we hide the purging.
Opacity is how to swallow real life,
A way to muddle all the verity.

Writing is basically
when existence gives you no choice
but to tell everyone a version
of your story.
And being published
is when someone decides
you are good at pretending,
believing you might appeal
to a particular sort of phony.

The Ways of a Man

Apologies

I apologize for my hair.
Maybe I'll get it twisted
when I make more money.
Maybe I'll cut it
to please my parents.

I apologize to my wife.
He hath gone awhoring after other gods
real and imagined.

And I apologize for the Yankees.
There really should be a hard cap.
Lately,
doesn't seem to help 'em much anyway.

I apologize
Lie prostrate on the floor
Rend my clothing
Wear sackcloth
and cry aloud
for Florida 31,
Mississippi State 38.
That loss was sacrilege.
I did not wear my rally cap.

I apologize for more friends than enemies.
I apologize for being lukewarm.
I apologize for cowardly discretion
Nobody can serve two masters.
I have saddlesores from the fence.

I apologize for 10 percent of my CD's.
I apologize for bad credit.

I apologize to my grandmother.
I know you see me.
I'll never see the pulpit
being this sorry.

Victoria's Secret Jeweled Citrus

I am recalling
how your damp bare sierra
blushed
at the pressure of touch
how I moved you with the motion
moistening you with lotion

I am reveling
in the pleasure of cadence
my comfortable arrhythmia
seeing you sway
a sinuous
private
pendulum

I look at you
when we are alone,
on morning afters
after showers
when I am privileged to see you
new, even, and floral
and believe already you are
much of the woman
you will grow to be,
that there is little for you
to come into,
that all of the surprises will be pleasant
and I can trust what I see

I won't wander off into daydreams,
reminisce about the pleasure
of sincere and devoted half-naked embrace,
about how water evaporated
from the crests of your curves
about how you would rest on my chest,
fragrant
and wearied by respiration's repetition
because you'll always be there,

even after it's not
new, even after the youth we possessed
no longer makes us graceful and sexy
when age makes us sages
and we are not daunted by beauty

For now though,
while anything we do is phenomenal,
you sit in my lap
little, like your kisses on my neck
and I breathe in your scent
run my fingers through your hair
my hands down the extent of your legs
and over the fall of your breasts
For a moment
I want to consider the contrasts,
imagine that I am patient,
pretend that I can envision control
through such exquisite haze.

Momma Home

tonight i had the back of your upper arms
in my hands
i kissed you
as you sat in the chair
you were otherwise engaged

your hair was on my face
i kissed your shoulder
came around to your side
bent to kiss the skin
above the lace of your camisole
nudged it so i could kiss lower
but your momma was home
i spread your fingertips
my hand over your hand
and watched the screen disappear
into your eyelids
just as
"mo-
ments
in love"
stopped downloading

your mother must've been home

you flashed me and told me to leave
your underwear was aquamarine
you remained otherwise engaged
yo momma must've been home

...better yet, newlyweds

I am waiting for her to come in.

I am half submerged, seething
daydreaming about childhood
in the tub, remembering
how I used to be afraid that my melanin
was floating to the top in the dead skin
'cause the water seemed browner
the more I slumped.
I remember telling my momma
that baths were pointless,
'cause you really couldn't tell if I was dirty
or if all the brown cake stuff
was soap-bleached skin.
My brother had a habit
of putting the rag in his mouth
no matter where it'd been.

When she comes in
I barely open my eyes,
I love when she's like this.
By now, she knows
I think she's pretty with no clothes on;
You can see it in the nonchalance
with which she does anything
that requires bending
or turning her back to me.
I notice for the millionth time
that everything beautiful about her
is bell curved or crescent shaped.
She glares playfully at the pen and pad
placed a safe distance from the tub,
gets in behind me and snaps
"Stop trying to be a poet for a minute
and let me wash your back."
Anyway,
I've known her for years,
But we've only been at this for days,
and while she gets down by my waistline
like its always been this easy
I find it gleefully difficult to pretend
that I'm used to it.

Opportunity Cost

I still see the angle your legs made
on the bed when I walked in,
how you adapted them
to hold a thick ethics book.
The evening sunlight so tempered
by half-turned blinds
you needed a potpourri candle,
your track thighs in those short shorts,
the red toenail polish.
Long black hair with brown streaks,
and something I'd written
tacked into the wall over your head.

I know you were just waiting on me.
We both had somebody,
both needed to be rescued from certainty.
Audacity in the moment
can change a life, but I was timid,
and so everything has happened
for a reason.

in memory of a dark girl

I am missing you a little,
More than I thought,
and more than I should.
But your spirit hovers over me.
Impish.
You must stop playing with my halo.
I should stop letting you.
Shoo, gone now.

You know me well.
It was the melanin, I'm afraid
It was watery,
It leaked all over you.
No mixing, no adulterating.
Grain alcohol blackness
saturated even the tangled,
sovereign curls
you idly twisted in daydreams
It simmered on your cheeks,
a veiled emotion.
It seeped onto your breasts,
where it burst at their conclusions.
It dove into your lips, where…
Those lips.
Your lips were grey.
They were like black
after pink lost out.
They were softly
corrugated and nice.
Your tongue was neon
against night's background
It was easy to see between teeth.

You were better for shadow
like poems for solitude
The bad lighting to finish good novels to,
There were secrets in your stare
that made it worth the strain to see you
I could you make you out
in basements with no light.

I could feel for the warmth
that had blown out the bulbs,

and follow the heat of an urge
that could rip out a pull string

Or you would usher me down,
slowly
compelling exploration
until I could not stay
the night.

the imprints

I don't really mind you
you burden me different
you walk like you think you could hurt something
your toenails still have the night before's
glitter on them, so pretty

early in the morning,
while people write postcards
and choiring birds wake up
earth's angels and devils,
your languid, brooding massage
soothes me before the pummeling.

I don't know, maybe you have wider spaces
between your toes,
but there is so much more of me
clinging to your feet
by the time you get to the chairs

Mistress Summer

sleeveless tees
adidas flip-flops
and you in a dark mood

feel you in my hair and on my skin

I touch you more now
trying to make new love
pressing the car past 60

I let you follow me home
knowing that you're a flirt,
certain that you'll go away soon
contentious and moody

all day you rage red-faced
acting so sweet now
but you don't love me
you just do what you do

still I can't help letting you
in through the windows all night
even past when the crickets go quiet.
Sometimes when I'm in bed
I feel your breath on the covers
so I sleep without the sheets
to keep you satisfied.

I guess I never have been able
to hold back-
Some night this winter you'll show up
just to surprise me,
whispering warmth,
and I'll meet you on the porch
like that weekend we had in Wilmington

dressed in my night clothes,
waiting in a canvas beach chair
with a plastic cup
and the wires of my stereo speakers
snaking Marvin Gaye
beyond the sliding glass.

Slow Dance

Soundtrack: 1. Slow Dance (R. Kelly)/ 2. Slow Jam (Midnight Star)/ 3. Red Light
Special (TLC)/ 4. Slow Dancing in a Burning Room (John Mayer)/ 5. Wildflower
(New Birth)

Tonight,
lest she become merely

a quick tremor of air,

and because she is something
he wants to learn

Assiduously,

palms press lightly
over the taut swale of arch,
the pressure of fingertips
up and down seeking
a rhythm from the slender shoulders
to the strait of her spine
like something sought for
in a dark room
hurriedly
Desperately

the closeness of her embrace
testifies to comfort
a young faith
in the sudden discipline of hands
fretting soft scratches of need
into the neck of her mandolin hips

and there is no governor for the heart rate
the breastplate is merely translucent
breathing is rationed to achieve cool
trying to convince her
the throbbing in his ribs
is a false positive

but while her hand and head
rest on his shoulder
like *you are my lady*

and while a beauty mark
just over the rise of her lip
is a dark moon
easily eclipsed and revealed
by teeth

and while the shea butter scent
of dark revolutions
inhabit his temple
like praise
the man knows
he has not been able
to stop the swoon

hasn't managed
the depth of the dive--

Preferring to yield
to a useful sort of weakness,
Anxious only for the notion
of the moment passing
uneulogized,
a mind absent the memory

How her body
was the contour
of a craving

Pretty Woman

She likes to know
she's beautiful,
doesn't mind men
with swift eyes.
Her mercy is sufficient
for accidents.

Sundresses helplessly
radiate thighs,
Conceited camisoles
arc russet shoulders
through a dark clamor
of hair.

The ring reins in
his fingers.
If I watch
what I want
he imagines,
I can keep what I need.

Marrying Up

The apples are in the bottom of the fridge,
she says.
You don't look for nothing.
He has already looked there
Once.

As still as she lies on the couch
reclined on her side
air drying over a towel
she must be the subject
of a nude
a likeness in the eye
of some would-be Wyeth
in the television.

I'mma get Food Network taken off the cable.
Ain't seen nal' bit of evidence
you learnin' anything.
Down in the crisper,
plump pomegranates
cover up the Cameos.

Butterflies (for Milly)

He just be a-talking don't he?

Can't hear you.
Whatever you said in response,
We agree.
We sit beside each other close
I'm glad we got to this point

PYT
You young like *Air Forces*
laced up with the top holes showing,
Extra strang tucked
behind the tongue.
Tell me something.

here she go…

True. Couldn't quite hear, but
Yes. Yes to whatever you just now said.
I like it when you do that
Right there Right there.

Your perm
inadvertent on my cheek
Your breath on my face
What else can I ask you?
What other ruse can I invent
To be close to your smell

And how to say I am high
off very recent curling iron, very recent
How to say to my sisters who kept naturals
This sensation cannot be touched
There is nothing like that heat
I do not mind did hair

I love this period.
I don't ever wanna change class.
He can talk all day.
(God, that smell all day)
When he gone show another film?
I mean
I can think of so much to say

There are so many
shoulder-length reasons for breathing you in

and if you would hear me,
you must listen to me
just before I speak,
when I push through slowly
to savor your scent
and brush against your cheek
to say something at your ear
I have something to show you
and somewhere
where no one is watching
because nothing is untoward in private
I wish you could talk to me
Purposefully
the way you accidentally do,
like how I'm trying to talk
to you.

Like When I Spot a Rainbow*

more than once in awhile
I think about

hey
I was just calling to say
today there is the prettiest rainbow
outside

I was just thinking about you
It made me think about you
and… I don't know
anyway
call me later.
bye.

----

*From "Diamond in the Ruff," by Jaheim.

Summer

Gone and get brown while it's out;

Summer sun passes behind clouds
but it will be out again soon

for someone

try to be comforted
by the nice tan you got
once you come inside

drowning

I am looking for air
in a room full of breath
I am too tired of loss
to sleep

you,
always something to do
after all I can do
is done
an all day fearing that
I forgot something
and I know,
no pet names
too early
but
need you baby
need to hear
yes baby
by accident

wonder if there is a way
I could move inside you
to make you always remember
Imprint myself   cerebral
a wall I could lean against
a dust outline just my size
that couldn't be washed away
by the moon

Last night
my deep breaths came
only in thoughts
that I may not remember forever
that there is hope in the distance
Opiate and lotus
but in the closeness
there is too much proximity
I am scared sweetheart
I can never be well
so close to the source
and in case you recover
this is something
to flood me in

in case you keep it out
something you let
rub you red
absently
until you ache again

I want you wet like me
in a revival of recall
Come share my chest
Feel it tighten
do you know how it closes
over a heart in hiding
have you felt how it labors
when it yearns?

The Wife of Thy Youth

Drink waters out of thine own cistern, and running waters out of thine own well...
and rejoice with the wife of thy youth... let her breasts satisfy thee at all times; and
be thou ravished always with her love. And why wilt thou, my son, be ravished
with a strange woman, and embrace the bosom of a stranger? For the ways of a
man are before the eyes of the Lord... Proverbs 5:15, 18-21

do you remember
the convenience of tinted windows
how I reached over
to kiss you at stoplights
in parking lots

the thump of the Kenwoods and JVC's
just wantin' to be seen witcha man
in a loud car, no headaches
my noise and my passenger seat
in our city
being the shit

tiny stars in the white space
of a cartoonish thought bubble
just before you know
you will give yourself over
to loneliness and sweat and attraction

how we glimmered with anticipation
smiled in disbelief

do you remember kissing
in a foreign tongue?
Remember it baby, or
Lately, perhaps
you can only imagine it possible
imagine having a reason
to reach over at night
being cupped and pressed together
'til we run over
Urgent hands laden with possibility
loving like a keepsake
you'd have to give back

once there was a moment
we were separated

only by an instant of audacity
and I thought I just leaned in
as you stood in the doorway
trying to leave and trying to stay
or were we so caught in the moments
we never took notes

was there ever a time we fucked
in the back seat of a compact car
like we lived at home
and had part-time jobs
or didn't work at all

why didn't I get tint in the new ride,
was I so old?
and was I ever so gone
off some you
a younger you
that I dreaded the thought
if you give it to me
like this here
you'll give it to others like-

where are my fig leaves?
who knew there was more to know
were you a pretty little dangerous thing
come to remind me of vertigo
where is your name charm now
and did your lips and breasts
smell of young sex like
green apple jolly ranchers
and candied lip gloss
remember me
being so weak
making it so inevitable
so certain a cascading
down a slippery slope
toward a sinful sort of novelty that-

Was it you baby?

Remind me,
don't let me forget,
they say it get like
that sometimes but

Was it you?

That was you, right?

Or was it

Somebody else?

Having a Mistress

I do not want what I haven't got. - Sinead O' Connor

You simply cannot go around
telling everyone you think is cute
that they're cute,
and this is especially the case
if one is married.
There is a certain tact a man has
who doesn't want to lessen his chances
of having an affair
with any one woman
by flirting with too many women.
But as my wife points out,
this sort of dilemma,
this trouble with making
prospective mistresses feel equally special
is a problem
only sorry men have.

I don't have a mistress
because they're hard to get,
and to get one
would mean I could get more,
or perhaps have to choose
between several I could dally with
plus the wife and
what if it's hard to decide?

If a woman is worth my dallying with,
She deserves more than dalliance,
She deserves permanence.

Unless she's happy with dalliance.

Which is a moot point, because
I have permanence and I'm happy with it.

The problem with permanence
is that it never gets new-unless you count
how it becomes different as it ages.
Some get a big rewarding kick out of this.
Overall, you feel permanence is enough,
but everyday

you see someone that makes it, umm
maybe not so good.
But you really are happy,
and there's only so many people
crazy enough to be with one person
Permanently.

We are bound
to get into foreign entanglements.
I feel like a cheat when I do
and a punk when I don't.
But I remember the big picture.
I don't need the entanglements,
I need permanence.

When I am famous,
which would mean
things were going well in a way,
I imagine she'll be interviewed
And my wife will say
I know he's very happy with me.
I am also certain
that he wants to cheat on me
Constantly. I am nearly as certain
that he never has and never will.

Granted,
this may not be her answer.
Maybe this is my answer
for her.
I have never been
what I thought I should be.
I should not be specific.
Specificity isn't what one does
who is hoping for a therapeutic benefit
in generalized acknowledgement.
And thus, no specifics
are provided.

Reconstruction

The lights go out down the hall
and they come in,
just when I'm nearly done
folding my clothes,
right before I can get away.
She puts the baby down
and mentions that my eyes are a little red.
"Tired," I say.
"I'll get over it."

But I think I say it too quickly,
like a reflex.
In our platform bed,
an approximation of something at Ikea
we can't afford,
I gallantly poise my body over the edge
to set the alarm.
Then I dab my eyes with the sheet
and stare at the wall, as if
the disembodied hand of a mean teacher
is showing me right-hand slant.

At the foot of the bed
the little one toddles by,
wobbling and recovering.
Her head half-blocked
by the sunny orange top
of a sippy cup,
I notice one eye fixed on me,
a slight smile like she's hip to things.
Then she laughs,
tipsy with ignorance,
and hurtles through the doorway
into the hall.

A Few Years In

For now,
I've brushed the leaves into a corner
to remember how the patio looks.
I open the screen door
to yell for approval.

On cold nights
the air smells scoured clean,
and even in the city
the sky darkens just enough
to see stars.
I point out the orange moon
and hold her like the male lead.
When I squeeze too tight
she never pushes back
like she needs room.

Sometimes I show love like
I don't want her to wonder
if there's anything more to know.
Every so often in the stillness,
More work comes down
around us.

Creative Control

Pushy little thing stretched mama's middle
until it softened into a home,
and so begins immersion in a new world,
gently mandated reading on natural birth
and breastfeeding and soy versus cow

Then the walking and talking starts,
and for all the handpopping at electrical sockets,
the shushing during TV shows and church,
a bitter retreat from the entrenchments
of what you said you wouldn't tolerate begins

hard to resist her little face
hard to deny the potency
of those mildly vinegar,
ever slipper and sockless feet
In the cartoon Caillou learns to ride a bike
so she lies on her back and mimics him pedaling
getting carpet in her pony tails

so funny, except the kicking reminds me
of how she buffets our restraining walls
and bucks against our reins

Soon it'll be time to agonize
over mission statements and curricula
The cost of the Montessori daycare
The Lutheran versus the Presbyterian preschool
application packets with sample aptitude tests for two year olds
an evaluation sheet full of decisive adjectives
some demigod circles for a living

All this time with Grandma
we could count on little worse than the comforting
bemusement of cartoonish Hallelujahs
and sudden snatches of gospel songs
Now who knows what she'll come home with
Children hodgepodged together
Their tidy orbits around their parents pulled out of shape
by an attraction to objects their own size,
offered gluttonous new grab bags
of attitude and opinion and influence
from different homes

Just imagine the correctness and falsehood
in how we'll smile at the meetings
and shake hands at the Christmas programs
knowing we're at home
trying to edit out the vestiges
of other people's kids
more than three days a week.

comfort woman (after Meshell N'degeocello)

baby, grab a bag
and put it in that pitcher
fill it up and put it in a chair on the porch
so the sun hit it

I put 2 cups of sugar in
too much for me
almost drowned out the tea

dinner is ready
homemade chicken soft tacos
and Trading Spouses

Could've done without
but I'll take it
she was sent here by the agency
they decided she was more perm than temp
the people here had no say
even HR is overseas

she is always on automatic pilot
can't lie sometimes I miss the turbulence

eight hundred dollars for two weeks of work.
our rent gets paid,
my whites still smell like Clorox,
and even the spot on the tee got spray and washed

The Proverbs
31
woman,
finally
gets around
to my button

Man I can't wait
watch when I'm able to take care of you
when I get money
we'll hide away
and only come out
to be a blessing

once you've given yourself so much to think about
it's nice, in a way
I guess
not really having to think
of all that much

I mean
the brush script is nice
but this new times roman
you can pull it up anywhere
you are always going to be this way,
right?
are you still waiting for me

gone outside,
I'm coming

the helpmeet
meets all

the household priest
ain't much help

so at least
I can be glad you're home
it's good to see you baby
how hard can it be
to kiss you
like you all I got

something for the road

This morning
daylight came contritely
to the heavy fringes of the curtains,
knowing it needn't do much
to stir anxious souls
unaccustomed to even short separations,
and we lay in our neutral corners
until
as if given a signal
you were into my side
kneading me into something you could spoon with
pressing against me
with something
for the road

About the Author

Cedric Tillman hails from Anson County, NC and was raised in Charlotte. He is a graduate of UNCC and The American University's Creative Writing MFA program. A Cave Canem fellow, Cedric's poems appear in several publications including *Crosscut, Folio, The Chemistry of Color, Cave Canem Anthology XII* and *Home Is Where: An Anthology of African American Poets From the Carolinas*, edited by Kwame Dawes. He lives in Charlotte with his family.